THRILLING MOMENTS
By Janis Da Silva

PRELUDE

Imagine meeting Michael Jackson, and spending some heartfelt moments with the superstar.

This book captures the wonderful adventures of a young lady who received that one in a million chance of a lifetime; the chance to get close enough to Michael to find out what millions wonder. It is the zany and delightful story about the sheer magic in making a dream come true, and finding yourself face to face with Michael.

The book also projects a special inspiring message about the key to success. It contains moment by magical moment in exclusive photos of Michael. The photos really help make the story vivid, giving the reader the feeling of being there in every episode. It's packed with excitement and laughs as the reader discovers what Michael's really like.

Published by
J.L. Tiffany Publishing

Copyright © 1987, J.L. Tiffany Publishing. All rights reserved. Copyright # TXu 275 819 under the alternate title: "Dreams Can Come True" and "My Weeks With Michael."

Reproduction or translation of any part of this work beyond that permitted by Sections 107 and 108 of the United States Copyright Act without the permission of the copyright owner is unlawful.

Printed in the United States of America

SR ADA 14-730474

874536

Although names of persons except for the author and the Jackson family and other public figures, have been changed to protect their privacy, and conversations have not been recalled word for word, the events portrayed in this book are substantially true, and were experienced by the author during her teen-age years in Chicago.

THRILLING MOMENTS

INTRODUCTION

Have you ever had a dream come true, or wished for something and it came to be?

The feeling you get from having that long-awaited dream come true or that fantasy come to life is very special, and should be remembered and cherished forever.

This book is dedicated to those that dare to dream. Hold on tight, and don't ever stop chasing those dreams. Always remember; "If you can dream it, it can happen!"

Now come, turn the pages and find out what happened when I decided to make my dream come to life.

This book is dedicated in loving memory to my sister,
Angela Patricia Coleman.

Michael's Encino estate.

Is this where you go Michael? When all the glitter is taken off, and the costumes are neatly packed away, behind this gate a busy, creative giant is dwelling, and when he comes out, he is sure to quench your entertainment thirst, and at the same time leave you wanting more. We've all seen Michael, the world-famous and sometimes controversial adult. Now let's meet Michael as I once knew him — Michael, the boy next door.

*Michael as I first knew him.
A page from my own personal photo album of memories.*

THRILLING MOMENTS

Looking up at the cheerleader list posted outside the gymnasium, I noticed my name was not up there. "Well, if it isn't Janis, too bad you didn't make the team." A voice came from behind me. I looked and it was Alicia.

Alicia was the prettiest and shapeliest girl on the cheerleading team, and believe me she knew it.

"I must be going," I smiled as I rushed down the hall. Alicia was about ready to rub my nose in the fact that I didn't make the team, and I didn't want to hear it. "Hi Bridget," I smiled as I walked into my biology class.

Bridget sat in front of me in class; she is my best friend. She's a little radical at times, which makes her so much fun.

At home that evening, Bridget and I, as usual, are talking to each other on the phone. "Janis, that Alicia is always picking on you. I would like to shut her mouth, once and for all." "Bridget, she hates everybody. I think she is jealous ," I replied! "Jealous of moi," Bridget joked. "I'm serious, Bridget. You are very pretty, and everyone likes you. Plus, you're in charge of the student newspaper." Bridget laughed, "Well, that's true! But I still do not like the way she laughs at people and talks about them." Bridget went on to say, "You know what Janis, I've been thinking, I would like you to be my assistant on the student newspaper. That would really shut her up but good." I replied excitedly, "Bridget, I would love to work with you, but not just to make someone jealous." "I agree 100%, but it will have its advantages," Bridget giggled.

The next day in biology class as I walked in I noticed Bridget was not there. About ten minutes after Mrs. Collins had started her lecture, in walked Bridget, who then proceeded to quickly sink down into her chair. Mrs. Collins briefly frowned at Bridget and then continued on with her lecture.

"I spoke to the principal, Janis, good news," Bridget whispered. After class Bridget turned around. "Janis, guess what?" Bridget beamed. "What!" I asked. Bridget started eagerly explaining, "I talked to the principal about you being my assistant on the student newspaper and he said 'Yes, of course!'" "Bridget!" I smiled with tears in my eyes, "I can't believe it, me, working on the student newspaper." "I'll call you about our next assignment as soon as I figure out some of the details." Bridget added as we departed in different directions. "Bridget" I replied, extending my hand. We shook hands and smiled. "Partners," I grinned.

Later that night . . .

"Telephone, for you, Janis," my brother Kevin called out, "Thank you," I replied as I picked up the phone. "Janis," Bridget's voice sounded extremely excited, "are you ready for this?" Bridget asked. "Yes," I answered, with my eyes widening as I sat down, "Go ahead."

Bridget began, "Janis, guess who is coming to town?" before I could answer the question Bridget blurted out, "Michael Jackson and his brothers!" "Everyone in school is crazy about them. Imagine us doing an interview on them for the student newspaper." Hearing the excitement in her voice I asked, "Bridget, are you serious, because I really didn't think this could ever happen?" "Yes, I think I have figured out a way to find them and get in to see them," Bridget exclaimed with confidence! "Are you sure," I questioned?

"Bridget, I have always dreamed of coming face to face with Michael Jackson. I mean, to look him in the eye, to see what goes on inside. Oh!" I gleamed with more excitement than before, "You're getting me excited. The mere thought of meeting Michael Jackson, but how?" I sighed. "I haven't worked out all the details yet, but, I'm sure that if they put on three shows here, they'll be in town at least five days. And, in those five days, they will probably need some musical supplies," Bridget explained. "True, I'm sure they will be visiting a music store" I agreed. "So, I must get busy. Tomorrow morning, I will start calling every music store on the Gold Coast, until I find out something," Bridget informed me as we said good-bye.

Later...
I fell asleep that night; my dream seemed so real, I will never forget it. I was standing in a small room, enclosed in a pink cloudy mist. I was wearing a dress made of the finest lace. The sleeves were made of lilies. The belt was embroidered with salmon colored baby roses. My hair was adorned with Baby's Breath.

A door opened slowly, and there stood Michael, wearing a light grey tuxedo. In his hand was one red rose. As he took my hand, he placed the rose in it. We danced, holding the rose, looking into each others eyes. Suddenly, the music stopped, and he kissed my lips, ever so gently, while disappearing into the mist.

> **... there stood Michael, wearing a light grey tuxedo. In his hand was one red rose.**

That Thursday morning I daydreamed through breakfast. As late afternoon grew near, it did not even bother me that I had not seen Bridget all day. I figured that she was busy calling music stores.

That night, I was asleep in my bedroom when I woke up hearing Bridget's voice from outside my window. "Janis, Janis," she called in a half whisper. "Shhh, I'll be right down," I whispered back while grabbing for my robe and slippers.

Once inside the house, I could not believe what my eyes saw. Bridget was wearing a big afro wig and some weird looking clothing. "What are you doing?" "Why weren't you around today?" I asked, holding back my laughter, "and where did you get that wig?," I asked as I busted into laughter.

We went up to my room . . .
Bridget began explaining, "Go ahead, laugh if you will, but I called about thirty music stores, and found nothing. So, I had to go out to a few music stores dressed as a rock star. I even had to buy these stupid guitar strings, just to get some information," Bridget replied while taking off the wig and combing her hair. "If my father caught me in this wig he would kill me," Bridget went on to say. "You may need an afro wig too," she mentioned. "Oh no, my father would never let me wear one of those either," I replied back looking at the wig. "It makes people think you have something to do with music," Bridget encouraged. "I love the Jackson's, but I am not sure I want to look like them," I laughed. "Anyway, what did you find out today?"

> **"This was the lucky one," Bridget smiled . . . "**

"This was the lucky one," Bridget smiled, while handing me a business card to a popular musical supply store. "The lady said that the Jacksons come into her store, but I think she was talking about Tito and Jermaine, for their guitars. She mentioned that every time they are in town, it never fails, they stop in for something." "Bridget you are terrific," I smiled with enthusiasm, "Gee!, I don't look that bad," I went on as I tried Bridget's wig on, and looked in the mirror. We both giggled at the way I looked in the afro wig. "Now all we have to do, is go down to that music store Saturday, and wait. I'll get my brother Jeff to drive us down there; then we can follow them to their hotel from the music store," Bridget gleamed. "I'll bet they stay in one of those beautiful hotels on the Gold Coast," I added. "I can see us now walking in one of those places," Bridget smiled.

For the next few minutes, we both just sat there dreamy-eyed, thinking how wonderful it would all be. "I sure hope Michael likes me in an afro wig," I smiled. "I think he'll love us," Bridget confidently laughed. "But, not half as much as we love him," Bridget laughed and then added, "Please don't forget your camera. I'm going to borrow my Mom's. Well I'd better be getting home; see you in school tomorrow," Bridget smiled as she walked down the stairs; and I behind her, still in a daze thinking about meeting Michael Jackson. Before I could shut the door, Bridget stuck her head back in and smiled, "What a story this will make." "You're right," I smiled back as I closed the door.

Saturday finally got here . . .

About 9:30 a.m. Bridget and her brother Jeff drove over to pick me up. "Hi," I smiled getting into the car, "This car isn't very inconspicuous, being red and all." "Don't worry," Jeff added. We drove down to the music store and parked in the middle of the block behind a delivery truck. "This is great, we can see them, but they can't see us," acknowledged Bridget. "Unless this truck drives away, "reminded Jeff.

We sat there eating on popcorn for hours. Finally it was twelve noon. I think all three of us were tired and ready to give up when two black limousines pulled up to the music store. The car doors opened and a red haired man got out; then Tito, Jermaine, and Jackie followed him into the store. A few short minutes later, Michael, Marlon and four others got out of the other limousine and walked into the music store. By this time you can imagine how excited Bridget and I were. "It's them, it's really him," I smiled! "Did you see Michael," I added? "Did you see Jackie?" Bridget shrieked, "He's so fine." "They are all fine!" I screamed. Jeff just laughed at us. We waited about twenty minutes and then watched everyone get back into the limousines. We were able to follow them, which wasn't easy, because they took the scenic route. It was exciting following them. Finally, we followed them to a beautiful hotel with a red

The Jacksons Emerge from their Limos

plush carpet outside. The whole Jackson family was whisked inside the hotel, past some fifty screaming girls, standing just outside the lobby.

"Well girls, looks like you won't be able to get in to see them as easy as you thought," Jeff frowned looking at all the other girls. "Let's drive around the hotel, we need to know all the entrances," Bridget replied. We drove around three times. "Okay girls, call me when you want me to pick you up. I'm going home now, " Jeff announced. "Okay, Jeff," Bridget said while getting out of the car. "Thanks for everything," I smiled as I shut the door. "Good luck girls, and please be careful; that building is heavily guarded," Jeff reminded us as he prepared to drive away. Bridget and I looked at each other in dismay. We were just about to pack up our dreams and head for home when suddenly I noticed a revolving door. One guard was sitting there, and then all of a sudden he wasn't there anymore. Now he did not get on the elevator. We did not see him walk through the lobby. There was no way he could have disappeared like that into thin air. We waited and watched; he never reappeared. "Come here," I nudged Bridget. We walked across the street, and from behind a tree we watched that revolving door. The wallpaper in the hotel was an abstract design. "There it is, a door," I smiled, as the guard reappeared! The secret door was well blended into the wallpaper. You really wouldn't notice it unless you knew it was there. Now we had an edge on all those other fans. We knew something they didn't, a secret passage door. The guard smiled, and we just smiled back. Finally he walked over to the hotel desk, to talk on the phone, turning his back to us for just a minute, and that's the minute we were waiting for. "Let's go," I whispered.

One, two, three, we were in the revolving door, through the secret door, and up the stairs; it all happened so fast, I didn't have time to catch my breath. Before we knew it we were on the fifth floor. Out of breath, I checked my camera; just then the door labeled "Fifth Floor: opened. There stood a janitor; he was smiling. "How did you girls get in here?," he asked in amazement. We didn't answer; we just widened our eyes and pleaded, looking scared but determined, "Please don't kick us out." "Girls," he smiled, "the Jacksons are on the twelfth floor; take the service elevator and good luck," he laughed, pointing down the hall to a door labeled "Service Elevator." Bridget and I looked at each other. We were so excited. "Thank you," we smiled. Bridget pushed the elevator button. "This is it, no turning back now," she exclaimed. Before we knew it, we were on the twelfth floor. As the door opened we heard a vacuum cleaner running. I peeked around the door, and a maid was cleaning the hall. She turned off the vacuum as we approached her. "Hi," Bridget smiled and asked, "Do you know what room the Jackson Five are in?" "I just work here, I really . . . Well," she smiled. "We would really like to see them," I asked. "Please," Bridget added. We pleaded for a few minutes. The maid just stood there smiling. "Who is it you want to see?" A man's voice came from an opened door. Bridget looked at me and I at her. Mr. Jackson walked from behind the door, wearing a big grin.

"Who do you want to see?" Mr. Jackson repeated. "Michael," I answered. "Jermaine," Bridget answered. "I mean all of them," Bridget added. "How on earth did you two get past all that security? Well, if you made it this far, let me see what the boys are doing. Come in and have a seat." He showed us to two chairs.

The room was filled with security guards; they all smiled at us, and said hello. I remember the red haired man they called Red; he was their private bodyguard. Mr. Jackson walked back in, still smiling. "Now, if you want to see them, this way, ladies." As we got up, Bridget and I gave Mr. Jackson a kiss on the cheek. "Thank you," we smiled, as we walked into an adjoining television room.

"Who Do You Want to See, "Mr. Jackson Smiled.

The room was plush and fit for a king, with beautiful velvet chairs, and royal drapes with slashes on each side of the window, which had a lovely view of the garden. Marble statues set the decor, the kind you would find in a castle. There they were: Michael, Marlon, Tito, Jackie, and Jermaine, just kicking back, being themselves. They were laughing at a television program, called "Bozo." "Come on, girls, give the boys a kiss," Mr. Jackson laughed, and a roar of laughter came from the left side of the room, where we noticed about three or four more security guards.

Bridget walked over to Jermaine. The guys got up, and she kissed each one of them on the cheek, and they her. I just couldn't move. I was frozen, and then even the security guards said, "Come on, don't be shy." I slowly and shyly walked forward and kissed them one by one. It was like walking through a fantasy. They each smiled and returned the kiss, ever so gently. I remember how soft Michael's lips were and how good he smelled; his eyes were big, beautiful and honest. His skin was like silk, he was perfect. The guards started clapping and saying "Oooh Wee." It might sound silly but Bridget and I vowed to never wash our faces again.

> **I remember how soft Michael's lips were and how good he smelled; his eyes were big, beautiful and honest. His skin was like silk, he was perfect.**

We were offered a seat. We sat down very quietly and watched television. Everyone kept giggling at the program. After the show was over, I turned around and Marlon was at the table eating. They offered us something to eat. Bridget and I were really too nervous to eat. We just nibbled on some fruit to keep from being rude. Mr. Jackson was laughing about how Chicagoans hide and eat watermelon; it was very funny. After the food trays were all put outside for the maid, someone said, "Let's play cards." A game started. I remember the limousine drivers walked in and the game really got interesting. Bridget and I watched. It was exciting to see Marlon play; he was very good and very serious. He made the game fun to watch. I remember laughing at the way he intimidated the other players. I kept pinching myself to make sure I wasn't dreaming. A little voice in my head kept saying, "are you really here or is this a dream? Now if it's a dream, why can't I wake up?"

Meanwhile, Michael was in and out; one minute he was standing near you, and the next he wasn't. He was playing a game with us, I thought. "Let's get a picture of that," Bridget nudged me, pointing to an opened door. It was Tito in an adjoining bedroom playing his guitar. The drummer was with him, humming some kind of beat. I took this picture but his back

Tito was Practicing His Songs

was turned. "You heard it first," laughed Tito, as he turned around. We stood there about 15 minutes, listening to him play. It was beautiful being personally serenaded by Tito Jackson.

Walking down the hall was Jackie. "Oh no," he cried, but it was too late; I'd already snapped his picture.

Oh, no. You're too close for this picture!

"You're too close, next time make sure you have enough distance," Jackie lectured. "I'm sorry, Jackie, " I replied. "He smiled and started asking us questions. "How is school?" "Fine, we have finals next month," Bridget replied. "I know how it is, but you'll do all right?," he winked. "I plan to," Bridget smiled. Jackie was so down to earth, so nice, I couldn't believe how nice he was. He spoke in a very high, lovely pitched voice; it sounded like he was singing when he talked. "Did you drive down here?," he asked. "Bridget's brother drove us," I replied. "Where do you live?," he went on to ask. "Here in Chicago on the southeast side, a placed called Chatum," I answered. "Uhhum," he nodded. We stood there for a minute; he just kept smiling. He looked so very handsome.

"Hi, may I see your camera?" Michael shyly asked.

Michael Singing Down the Hall to Us

"I Love you, ooh, ooh," we heard Michael singing down the hall. As we turned around, "Mike," Jackie laughed, "what are you singing?" Once he knew we were watching he did a little dance while walking toward us. "Hi, may I see your camera?" Michael shyly asked. Bridget nodded yes. Then he walked up and gently took the camera from around Bridget's neck. "35 millimeter," he smiled; it seemed he knew a lot about cameras, looking it over like an expert. "It's my Mother's; she gave me a crash course on how to operate it yesterday, but I want to learn more about them," Bridget confessed. "Michael just smiled at her, handing her the camera back. "Cameras are interesting," he went on.

Jackie, Michael, Bridget, and I walked into a room where Jermaine and Randy were sitting; the view from the window was spectacular. "Michael, can I take a picture with you please?" I asked. "Wow, she talks just like the models in New York," his eyes lit up as he handed the camera to Jermaine. Jermaine took this picture.

"Thank-you," I smiled at him. He just smiled back. Michael turned toward me, and we looked into each others eyes for a moment, neither one of us saying anything. I wonder if he knew

Janis and Michael

how much I loved him; it didn't really matter, this moment was ours, and it was just the way I dreamed he'd look into my eyes. Michael and I just stood there looking out the window for fifteen minutes, not saying a word; it was so special. He seemed to be a thinker and a dreamer; what a lovable person he was.

Bridget went over to Marlon after he had finished playing cards. The two of them were talking for about a half an hour, but later I found out Bridget had done most of the talking. Before leaving the room I took a few pictures of Randy, Jermaine and Marlon.

Randy, Jermaine and Marlon relax in their hotel rooms.

Bridget and I started walking around just mingling, trying to get some good pictures of everybody and with everybody. We walked into a room where Tito was; I walked up and started asking him questions. "Where do you go to school when you're on the road?," I asked. "We have a tutor who travels with us," Tito replied. "Just one teacher for all of you?" I went on. "Yes, Rosy Fine, our tutor, she's great," Tito smiled. "In California do you go to private schools?" I asked. "Yes, but some of us go to public schools too, Fairfax," he answered. "Where do you live?" I asked. While he wrote down his address, Bridget took this picture.

Tito gives me his address

"If you're ever in California, drop by and say hello," Tito replied, giving me his address. "We may do that one day, but for now I'll just write," I smiled. "That's good," Tito smiled as I put the address in my pocket. I couldn't believe it. Tito Jackson had just given me his address. He was so down to earth. I didn't know who I loved more, Michael, Tito, Marlon, Jackie, Jermaine, or Randy. The decision was hard; they were all so handsome, so nice, so lovable, and they all smelled so good too. The whole twelfth floor smelled of Aramis cologne. I remember looking at them, watching them talk and laugh with one another. The relationship as brothers was fun, they enjoyed life and each other. They also enjoyed their fans, as long as the fans were not trying to rip off their clothes or something silly like that. Bridget and I felt so comfortable with them, like being with old friends we had known forever. Michael really projected warmth and kindness.

It was getting close to time to leave. We said our good-byes to everyone. While walking towards the elevator, we heard the drummer talking about the after-concert press party. "Sunday night?" questioned Bridget as we stopped walking. "Yes, you girls should come. I'm Tito's cousin." He offered his hand. Bridget and I shook his hand. "What time?" I asked. "After the concert," he replied. "We will try to make it," I smiled back while turning to push the elevator button.

"Wait for us," Michael's voice whispered across the hall. They had all changed clothes. "I've got to get some more pictures of them in those new clothes," I whispered to Bridget. Their security guards were with them. We all got on the elevators together. When we reached the lobby, Bridget and I went into the hotel store to get change to call Jeff to pick us up. I was buying some gum when they all walked in, smiling and laughing. Bridget went to call Jeff, and I just started snapping these pictures.

> "Shopping with the Jacksons; are you jealous?" . . . I guess I was acting prideful, but then it's not every day you get to go shopping with Michael Jackson and his family.

The Jackson's Go Shopping

Bridget came in just as they were leaving. "What were you doing?" Bridget looked surprised. "Shopping with the Jacksons; are you jealous?" I laughed. Mr. Jackson heard me and I remember him laughing at me. I guess I was acting prideful, but then it's not every day you get to go shopping with Michael Jackson and his family.

"Janis, why don't we exchange blouses and then take a few more pictures with them so we won't look the same on all the pictures?" Bridget whispered to me. "Okay, but this turtle neck will ruin my hairdo, getting it over my head," I reminded Bridget. "That's okay. Your'e wearing a wig, remember. Hurry!" Bridget smiled.

We rushed off into the ladies' room and exchanged tops. When we came out I took about three pictures of Bridget and Marlon with her camera, and she took this of Marlon and me after I had changed back again.

Bridget snapped this picture of me with Marlon

Caught in the Act

At the Concert the next afternoon . . .
The music began to play; and thousands of girls screamed and pushed their way to the stage. Finally, the guards got the girls under control. Bridget and I sat there and watched. "This reminds me of those old clips you see of the Beatles concert," Bridget laughed. "I'm so glad we can go down and visit them any time we want to," I smiled. "Yes, can you imagine what these girls would do to know what we know." Bridget and I laughed as we took out our cameras and Michael started singing. It was a very exhilarating concert. Michael's moves seemed to defy the laws of gravity.

> Michael's moves seemed to defy the laws of gravity.

After the concert . . .
Bridget and I were waiting for my parents to pick us up. Bridget began to get this gleam in her eye. "What are you thinking?" I asked, knowing she was up to something. "Let's go to the press party!" Bridget exclaimed. "Bridget, we have class in the morning, and my parents would never permit it. Besides, I only have one more picture left on this roll of film," I reminded her, but I could tell Bridget was set on going.

My parents drove up and we drove Bridget home. "Bye, and thanks," Bridget waved to us as she closed the car door. Once she was inside her house we drove home. "You girls were pretty quiet," My dad mentioned as we reached home. "Just tired, Dad," I yawned, walking into the house. I can't wait to see those concert pictures you took," My mom smiled. "Okay Mom, good-night," I smiled, as I entered the house. I walked into my bedroom and closed the door.

I was just about to undress for bed, when I saw the headlights of a car flashing in my bedroom window. I looked out. It was Bridget getting out of a limousine. "What are you doing?" I whispered. "Janis," she whispered in my window, "I couldn't sleep, "I'm just dying to see what it's like at that press party. Come with me," she pleaded. "Whose limousine is that?" I whispered back. "It's my uncle's; he drove here from California," Bridget proudly announced. "Why did he let you drive?" I went on to ask. "Shh, everyone was asleep when I got in, so I kind of borrowed it," she giggled. "Neat car huh?" she went on to point out. "Are you crazy, you don't even have a driving permit, and what if your uncle wakes up and finds his car gone?" my voice raised a little. "Come on, don't worry, he told me he was going to let me drive it, sooner or later. This just happens to be a little sooner," Bridget laughed. "I don't believe this," I shook my head. "Janis, please, I don't want to go by myself; anyway, Michael will be wondering why you're not with me," she encouraged. "The only thing he'll be wondering is why we're not in straight jackets," I laughed. "Sure Janis," Bridget smiled. After about ten minutes I began to agree. "You really want to drive down there?" I asked, smiling. "Can you see us driving up in this limousine? You can even ride in the back. I'll be your chauffeur," she grinned. "Let's go, it'll be fun," Bridget encouraged. Looking at the limousine, "Okay," I smiled. "God be with us," I murmured as I climbed out of my bedroom window, leaving it open just enough for me to climb back in without waking anybody up. It was my first limousine ride, and I must say I enjoyed it at first. People were staring in to see who was riding in the back. I was a little nervous; neither of us had a license but I tried not to make Bridget nervous. We were driving down Lake Shore Drive, when I suddenly noticed headlights coming towards us. "Bridget, quick, pull over here; quick!" I yelled. Bridget spun the car off an on-ramp just in time. "We were facing on-coming traffic," I screamed. "Please take me home; I should have had my head examined for even getting in this car with you," I cried. "Okay," Bridget pleaded. "But we're almost there, she went on. "I'm sorry, Janis." "Yea, we were almost there all right, almost there in our graves." After calming down from the scare I said, "If you promise to drive extra careful; otherwise, I'm taking a taxi home, and if you had any sense you would too," I replied.

Bridget was crazy, but she was my best friend, and in those days a best friend was more valuable than anything. Bridget drove very carefully from then on and finally we got there. "Are you with the Jackson press party?" the bell cap asked. "Yes, we were invited," answered Bridget. We walked in with our cameras and went to the elevator, leaving the limousine with the valet service. Girls in the door were wondering who we were, and how we walked in, because they could not get in.

Once upstairs, the elevator door opened and all we saw were flashbulbs going off, and cameras going click, click, click everywhere — a Nikon firing squad. I finally saw Marlon walking down the hall after about twenty minutes. "Hi," he waved. I could see he was tired.

We just stood and watched; it was very interesting. "I honestly understand how tiring this business can be," I explained. "After putting on a show like that, they must be tired, but instead of resting, they have to come back here and get more cameras flashed in their faces and bombarded with questions," Bridget added, shaking her head. "Let's go home," we agreed, walking toward the elevator.

Marlon managed to wave good-bye to us through the crowded hallway. "I'm glad we came," I smiled as we stood on the elevator. "Yea, now we really know what goes on after that last song is sung and the concert's over," Bridget smiled. "Thanks for coming with me," she went on to say. "Sure, that's what friends are for; now please get me home safely," I laughed, feeling glad I came and happy Bridget and I were friends.

Marlon sees us off from the party

When I got home, I opened the window and climbed back in. There he was, my father, sitting in my room, with one of those looks on his face that make you wish you were never born. "Where have you been, young lady? It's after midnight." "Dad, I'm sorry," I cried. "You're grounded for two weeks," he ordered as he walked out of the room very angrily and shut the door.

That next day in school, I walked over to my locker, and a group of girls ran up to me. "Janis, did you meet them?" "What were they like?" "Did you kiss Michael?" Questions came from everywhere. "Bridget told us all about it," Adrian Mcpherson cried! "I . . .," I tried to answer them, but they just went on jumping and asking more questions excitedly. "What's all this excitement about?" Mrs. Romaine, my physical education teacher, asked as she gently pushed her way through the crowd. "Janis met Michael Jackson and went to his private press party last night," informed Brenda, a girl who hardly ever spoke to me until now. "Is that right? Wow! Did you take any pictures?" Mrs. Romaine asked, as her eyes lit up. Soon the hall was filled with teachers and students. I was about to answer Mrs. Romaine when the bell rang for the next class. "Sorry, late for class," I smiled, as I gently pushed my way to class.

I walked into my math class, and everyone clapped. "Gee, news sure does travel fast," I exclaimed as I sat in my seat! The whole class, including Mr. Daniel, was smiling at me. I felt weird, getting all this attention. Walking down the hall after class, I saw Bridget wearing dark glasses and signing autographs. "here she is, the lady that Michael Jackson kissed," Bridget applauded while walking over to me. But she noticed I was kind of shy about the whole thing. Later we walked away. "Bridget, you told everybody, and I haven't even had a chance to tell my parents yet," I moaned, "plus I'm grounded for two weeks." "Why?" Bridget asked. "My father was waiting for me last night when I crawled back in the window," I answered. "Sorry to hear that," Bridget patted me on the back, "but cheer up, because

> "... around here you're a star ..." Bridget was right; suddenly Bridget and I were superstars in school.

around here you're a star," Bridget laughed. "Just look at your fans. We are the closest they will ever get to Michael Jackson," she further encouraged.

"Did you parents know you were out last night?" I asked. "No, nobody at my house knew I was gone last night; however, my uncle did notice his limousine was a little low on gas this morning," Bridget said, as we looked at each other and busted into laughter.

Bridget was right; suddenly Bridget and I were superstars in school. Girls would buy us lunch and give us birthday presents when it wasn't even our birthdays. I now had a lot of friends who all wanted to be my "best friend." It was nice to be liked by everyone, even Alicia. I really enjoyed having all that attention at times.

A few months later.

Bridget and I were listening to record albums at my house. The phone kept ringing. "Janis, it's for you again, one of your fans," my brother Allan sarcastically remarked while handing me the phone. "Hi, Kathy. No, I don't know if Jackie's favorite color is blue, okay, ... sure, bye," I said as I hung up the phone and sat down. "Gee whiz," I yawned, "this is getting old fast." "Same thing at my house. My Dad is about to rip the phone out of the wall," Bridget agreed. "Yesterday, I was in the school library, and a girl I'd never seen before begged me, I mean begged, for the Jackson's address. Whew," I sighed. "They trusted us; we can not break that trust by telling everybody their address," Bridget frowned. "Besides, it would take all the fun out of it if we told everybody," I added. "But the girls don't understand," Bridget added.

The next year . . .
Bridget and I worked during the summer at a dress shop on the north side of Chicago. When school started, we took volunteer jobs, at Operation P.U.S.H., (People United to Save Humanity). This organization held an Exposition every year.

The Expo was a showcase of manufacturers from our community, as well as out of state. There were some big record companies. In addition, there were concerts with top of the line performers, such as Bill Cosby, Stevie Wonder, and many, many other big names, including the one and only Michael Jackson. These performers would come and volunteer their time and performances every year.

Bridget and I answered phones and gave out information on the shows, the times, location, and where tickets could be purchased. It was fun. We only worked two hours every evening, but we met so many people, some of whom today I see in movies and television. But still we were Michael Jackson crazed and that's who we wanted to see.

> **They were phone numbers of stars, including Michael Jackson's private phone number in California.**

One night at work Bridget came into my office. "Janis, guess who's here?" Bridget beamed. "Who?" I questioned, eager to find out. "Berry Gordy and his sons; they are touring the Expo privately. Come on," Bridget replied as she coaxed me out of my office. They looked good. We shook hands with them; it was quite a thrill. Mr. Berry Gordy looked so handsome. It was quite an honor meeting Mr. Motown himself. That same day the phones seemed to be ringing more than ever, with opening day being one day away. We still hadn't found out where the Jacksons would be staying. I remember running across a list of phone numbers; these weren't just ordinary phone numbers. They were phone numbers of stars, including Michael's private number in California, and all hotel reservation information for Chicago. We never found out where that list came from. It was on a xeroxed paper. Bridget and I couldn't wait to get home and call Michael.

At Bridget's house, I remember dialing the number to California. "Hello," Michael answered the phone. "Hi Michael, this is Janis, from Illinois. I ran across your phone number while working at the Expo; I hope you don't mind me calling?" I asked. "No, not at all, I'm really looking forward to coming to Chicago this weekend," he replied. "Everyone here will be so glad to see you and your brothers; by the way, how is everyone?" I mentioned, while Bridget was in the background saying "What did he say . . . what did he say?" Everyone's fine, Janis, thanks for asking, and how are you?" he asked. "Fine," I answered. "How's the weather?" Michael asked. "You may need a rain coat," I answered, then added, "The weather is beautiful now, but it rained on Monday." "Thanks, I know exactly what to wear now," he laughed. "Michael, I'll say goodbye now, and see you later," I giggled. "Okay Janis, take care, see you in three days," Michael closed. As I hung up the phone Bridget was about to die. "What did he say?" she repeated. "He said . . .," as I paused in excitement, "'How's the weather?'" "How's the weather . . . oh, oh, how's the weather?" Bridget repeated. "It was really him," I smiled. "He said he didn't mind me calling, and he said . . ., are you ready for this Bridget?" I paused. "What!?" she said as she grabbed her heart. "He said, 'see you in three days,'" I replied. Bridget and I were so excited we jumped up and down like a couple of crazy teenagers that we were. Bridget's father came into the den and asked, "Did you girls really just call Michael Jackson at his California home?" Yes, Dad, it was him," Bridget answered, still excited.

> "Did you girls really just call Michael Jackson at his California home?"

"You two are something else. Don't call too often. That can run up a very expensive phone bill; also don't be a pest," he reminded us with a smile. "We won't," Bridget agreed, and I nodded, "Yes sir." It was hard to keep that promise, but Bridget and I limited ourselves to calling only once a month. We had that number for a few years until we lost it. It was nice talking to him once in a while. He was a good friend to have, always encouraging us in every way. He was so instrumental to us in the way he gave unconditional friendship and love.

Saturday couldn't get here fast enough. We were on the bus at 10:00 a.m.; we reached their hotel by 11:00. This time they were in a different hotel and no girls were around. We walked right in and went up to visit them. Jackie was standing in the hall when we entered. "Hi girls, how are you? Mike," he called into an open room, "Guess who's here?" Michael came out and I smiled. "Hi." "Hi," he smiled back. "Michael, can I take a picture of you two?" Bridget smiled. "Sure," Michael smiled as he put his arm around me for the picture. After the pictures were taken he smiled at me, leaving his arm on my shoulder. Then he kissed my cheek. I stood there. Looking into his beautiful eyes, I wanted to kiss him back, but I was too shy.

> **Then he kissed my cheek...Looking into his beautiful eyes, I wanted to kiss him back, but I was too shy.**

Tito smiled and offered us a cigarette. "No thanks," answered Bridget, "We don't smoke."

They seemed a little surprised to see us; they were probably wondering how we kept finding them. They never asked, because the mystery was kind of fun. We all stood there giggling. "We are coming back at the end of the year for our regular concert tour," Jackie explained. "Good, we'll see you then," Bridget replied. As she winked at me, Jackie smiled. "We are leaving for an interview with a magazine publisher," Michael reported, as Mr. Jackson walked down the hall towards us. "Hello ladies, how are you?" Mr. Jackson smiled while pushing the elevator button. "Just fine; we thought we would come by and say hello, and welcome you back to Chicago," I replied. "That's very thoughtful of you," he smiled.

Two elevators came at the same time. We all got on and rode down. "Have a good day," smiled Michael, as their limousines drove up. Bridget and I went shopping and had lunch before taking the subway home.

On the way home . . .
"Janis, I love visiting them," Bridget smiled. "Isn't it great; they seem so happy to see us, so warm," I agreed. "They really make us feel like good friends," Bridget smiled. "We respect them; I think that's what they like about us," I added. Bridget smiled. "Yea, and the fact that we don't try to rip their clothes off, or take pictures without asking, or try to jump in the bed with them." What?" I blushed. "Come on, Janis, don't be so naive," Bridget laughed. "Janis, many girls in our place would have tried something by now, and lost all Michael's respect," Bridget smiled as we prepared to get off the train. "That's why I picked you to come with me in the first place. You're not fast like some of the other girls in school," Bridget added. "Michael is so respectful toward us too. Yes, he is the perfect gentleman," I added.

> We loved the different outfits they would wear; every year was like watching an all-male fashion show.

Every year, while Bridget and I were in high school, they would come to town and we would go by to see them at least twice a year. It was so much fun. We loved the different outfits they would wear; every year was like watching an all-male fashion show. We found out a lot of things about them, from what kind of hair conditioner they used to the cold medicines they preferred — all those little details that teen magazines loved to write about. I remember Bridget and I would read the teen magazines and laugh. I honestly understand today why Michael won't do much interviewing.

One thing I realized from being around them was something about success. It's something you have to set yourself in the direction for, and it's not just being rich and famous; it comes from within. Michael showed us that even if he had lots of money, he was still Michael, a loving caring human being. The brotherly love they shared for each other, the caring and respect they had for one another and the ability to work as a team, these things were the winning combinations behind the talent, which I believe is true success.

> ... he was still Michael, a loving caring human being.

The last year Bridget went to visit them I was away at college. About a week after she had seen them, she called and told me that they asked about me. When they heard I was away at college, they were very delighted to hear I was furthering my education. I remember getting goose bumps just knowing they had asked about me; it really was inspiring.

I am glad I knew Michael Jackson and his brothers, even if it was for just a short period of my life. The friendship we shared gave Bridget and me special memories which we will treasure forever.

Sometimes it's not always the quantity of time you spend with someone, but it is the quality of that time spent which constitutes those dreams coming true . . . and makes them well worth their chase.

Bill Cosby is a laugh a minute. Here he selected two childre
to participate with him. Bill Cosby was very active in helpin
P.U.S.H. I respect him for what he has proven; you do not hav
to talk dirty to be funny! There is no one like him.

Isaac Hayes dazzled our hearts with his beautiful music. I love watching him on keyboards. Today you can see Isaac doing a lot of acting; he is loaded with many different talents.

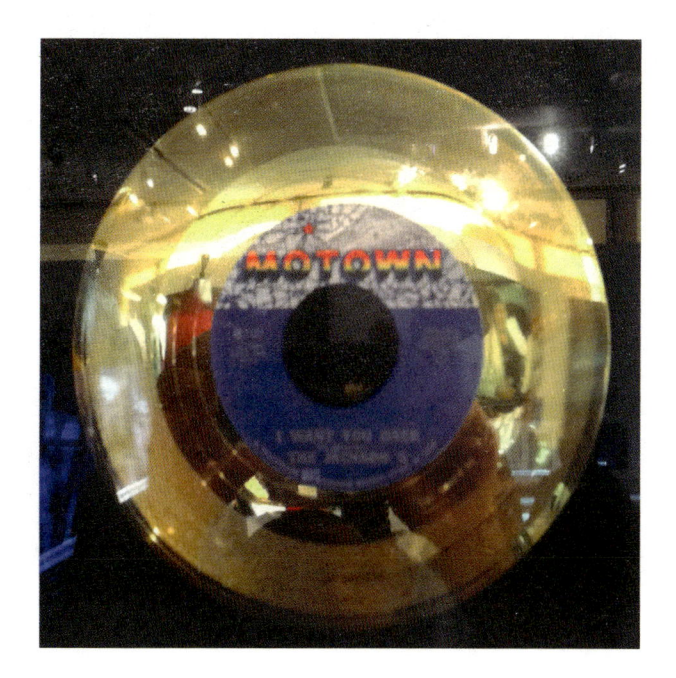

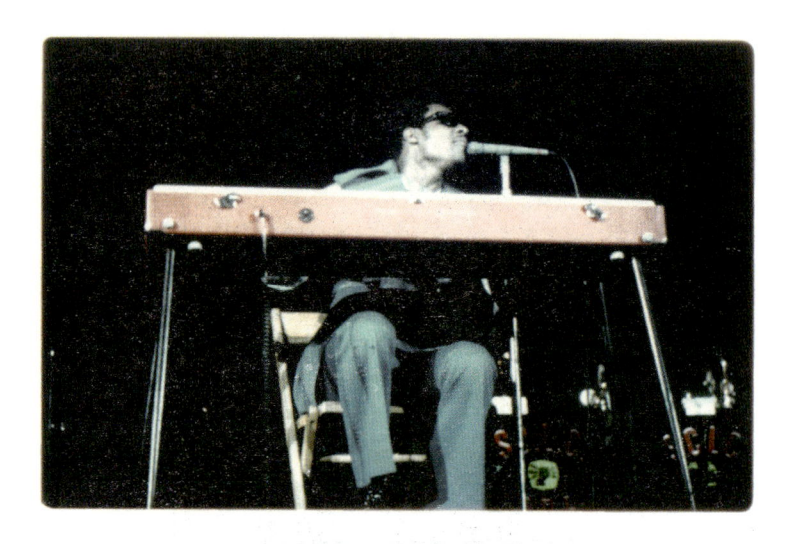

*Nobody wanted to miss Stevie
Wonder's performance*

Here we watched the Temptations

*Being with him year after year was **like** spending days in an amusement park because he is so much fun to be around. You never want to leave the excitement.*

Michael and Janis

When Michael says "he was sent here for the children," believe it, because growing up with him is one of the most exciting things a kid can have a chance to do.

Marlon and I stood here taking picture after picture. He was very polite.

The outfits were bright and cheerful

His smile sparks a special electricity.

Each step was done harmoniously

Once you're a Superstar there is just no privacy, even in going shopping.

Jermaine was finished shopping and ready to pose with a big smile.

After I finished college and had landed a wonderful job as a computer programmer, Michael hit the charts with "Off the Wall." The years prove to make him bigger and better than ever. "Thriller" thrilled millions as it brought excitement back into the music industry and sparked a new interest in the video marketplace. "The Making of Thriller" showed that Michael puts everything he has into his performances for his fans.

No matter how much bad press Michael gets, he has plenty of loyal fans who love his music and can't get enough of it. Thriller went on to break records all over the world, selling 40 million copies world wide. Pepsi even grabbed some of the excitement. Michael's Pepsi commercials are mini videos, representing a new generation, which is symbolic to his music.

Now, Michael is back with "Bad" a long awaited album, which is breaking records. Every song released from "Bad" thus far has become number one on the pop charts, as well as the black charts. It only proves once again Michael is truly an innovator and he is making history right before our eyes. It is nice to know I had that rare chance to watch him up close as we grew into this new generation.

USA for Africa, Camp Good Times, opening up his home to help others, the check he gave to the United Negro College Fund, these are just a few of the many ways Michael has given of himself. It also says he is still working to keep the dream and theme behind (P.U.S.H) People United to Save Humanity.

Michael went from the boy next door to Rock Star with the whole world watching, with millions of people expecting him to be perfect, and every time a flaw is spotted it hits the news.

Michael generates happiness. Once I was interviewed by a newspaper about how it felt to meet Michael. I told the reporter that I was excited, he was very nice, very polite. I met a person who was down to earth, yet heavenly. He is fun to be around because of his happy attitude toward life and his career. He loves his fans a lot, and love begets love. Of all the commandments, love is the greatest.

Now you have it — a look at Michael from a person much like yourself. Sometimes we get caught up in the media's interpretation of a famous person. Very seldom we see it from a non-media oriented aspect. So go ahead and dream. "Reach for the moon, because even if you miss, you will land among the stars." I did.

The picture above was taken September 14, 1990, at the inaugural installation of the Michael Jackson Good Scout Humanitarian Award. It was also the night Michael read this book. He loves the book so much, he called me up late that night to tell me so. We talked about the old times, and had a real fine conversation. He is a genuine friend, the kind you can go years without seeing or talking to and then when you finally do see each other the friendship picks up where it left off, as if it were only yesterday.

Michael.... Michael, I see you're about to board that plane. However before you go there is something you should know. Since this book has been in print (1987) I have been getting countless letters from my readers. On behalf of them, I must say, they love your voice. To them it is sweeter than the rarest bird's song, and truly a gift from God. Thanks for sharing it with us.

Well as Michael travels around the world creating those "Thrilling Moments", don't worry this writer will take the pen to write the words again.

ST0707 FLR 2 22 7 M-TYPE EST0707
EVENT CODE SECTION ROW SEAT ADMISSION EVENT CODE
0.00 FLOOR 2 0.00 CN 48942
PRICE
MICHAEL JACKSON
MEMORIAL SERVICE
TUES JULY 7, 2009 10:00AM
NO CAMERA/VIDEO/RECORDING
FLR 2
AC 5X
22 7
600MSTP
2JUL09
AC 470
FLR 2
600STP
22
0.00
7
650282998496
STAPLES Center

PLEASE HANG ON REARVIEW MIRROR
THIS SIDE FACING WINDOW
PLEASE READ BELOW
L.A. LIVE
STAPLES Center
NOKIA Theatre L.A. LIVE
DATE JULY 7, 2009
PRICE $ MJ
SPECIAL EVENT
LOT 1
LOT
(MAP ON BACK)
7000031108
7663
EVENT PARKING
Before you arrive at the Arena, remove the short stub from the parking pass and then hang the parking pass on your rearview mirror so it is clearly visible to traffic management and parking personnel before entering parking lots. Upon arrival, give the parking attendant the short stub.
Tear Here

Michael Jackson Montage: Coin necklaces, Turbo Powered Rolls Royce, History Pre-Release CD, Leatherbound Author Printing of Moonwalk.

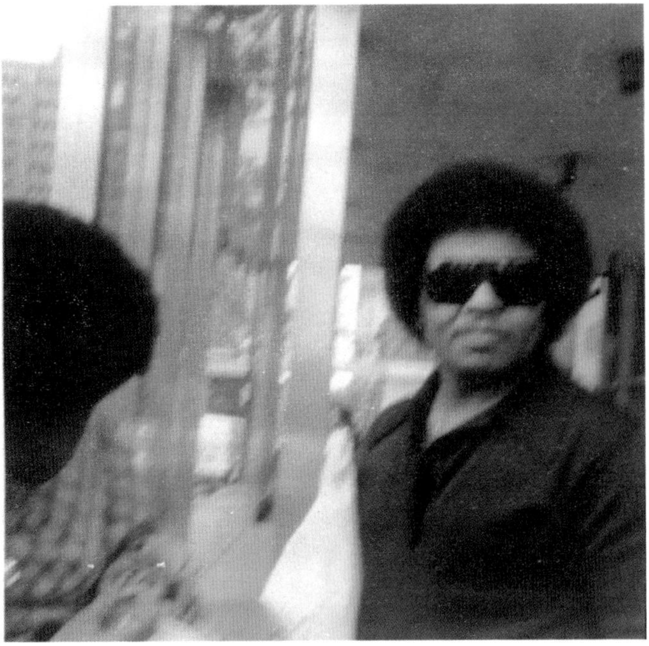

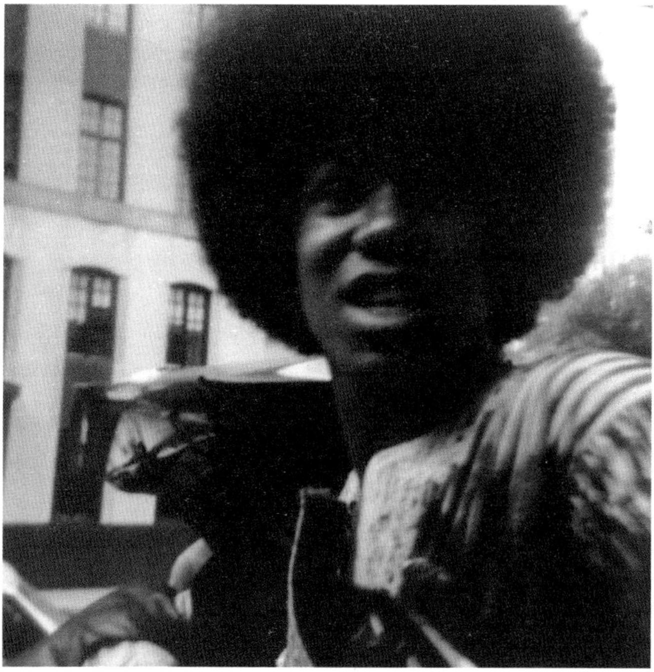

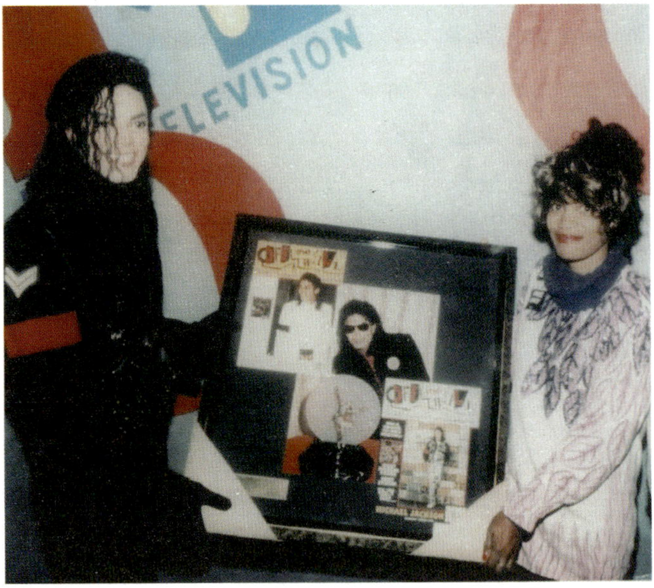
ELEVISION

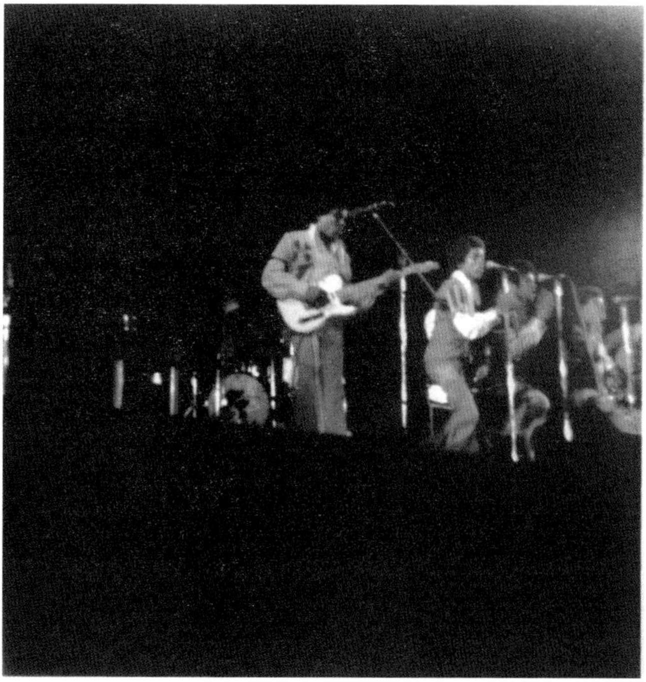

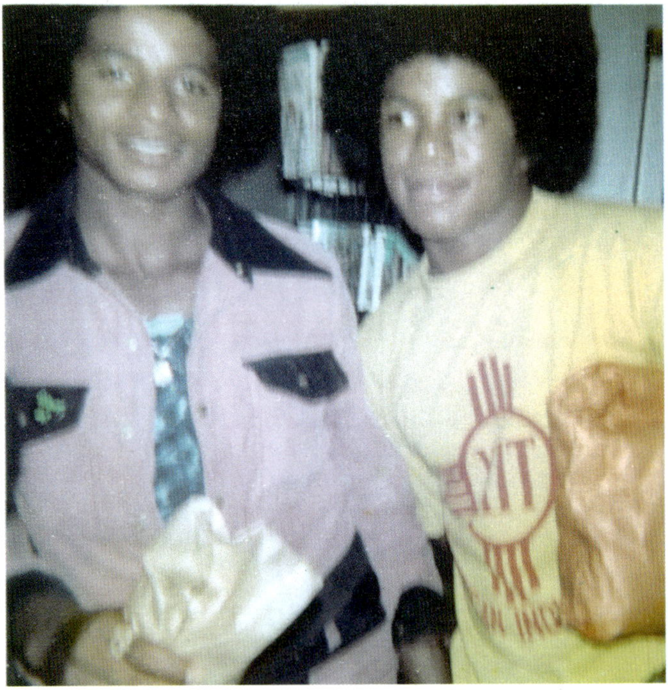

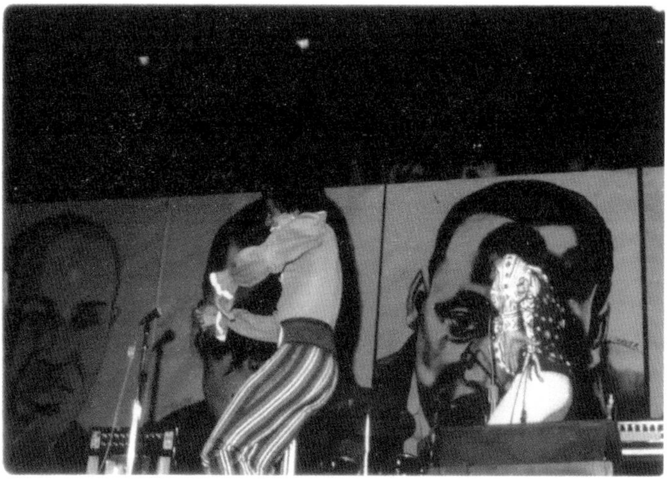

Janis Beneby da Silva

I am a true believer in God's word. I'm married, like having fun and doing the impossible. I love a challenge. Born in Northern Illinois, I graduated from college in Costa Mesa, California, with a degree in Business Information Systems.

I now live in California with my husband and my two daughters. I write and analyze computer programs for one of the largest data systems in the world.

I decided to write this particular book because this was one of the most memorable and thrilling times of my life, my experiences as a teenage reporter in quest of meeting a real superstar, Michael Jackson, finding out how he reacts off stage and out of the lime light, in his private everyday life, of just being himself.

Made in the USA
Lexington, KY
12 January 2013